# CHRISTIAN PRAYER AND LABYRINTHS

# Christian Prayer and Labyrinths

## PATHWAYS TO FAITH, HOPE, AND LOVE

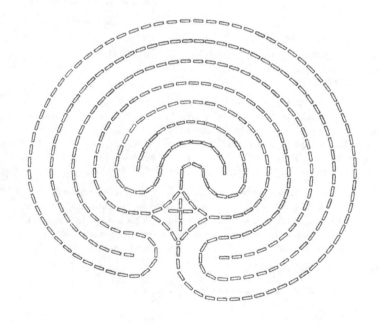

JILL KIMBERLY HARTWELL GEOFFRION

The Pilgrim Press  Cleveland

**DEDICATION** This book is dedicated to all those who have used, do use, and will use their vision, time, and energy to create and maintain labyrinths for communities of faith, including: LAUREN ARTRESS, ROBERT FERRÉ, and LISA GIDLOW MORIARTY

The Pilgrim Press, 700 Prospect Avenue, Cleveland, Ohio 44115-1100
thepilgrimpress.com
Copyright © 2004 Jill Kimberly Hartwell Geoffrion

Image of the Chartes Cathedral Labyrinth © 2003 Robert Ferré, used by permission. ·
Six line drawings of labyrinths by Lisa Moriarty, used by permission. · Drawings of
the Greek keys to a seven-circuit labyrinth by Jeff Saward, used by permission. ·
"Quick Introduction to Labyrinths" and suggestions for praying a labyrinth, cowritten
by Cheryl Dudley and Jill K. H. Geoffrion, used by permission. · Labyrinth journal
questions, cowritten by Elizabeth Nagel and Jill K. H. Geoffrion, used by permission.

Scripture quotations, unless otherwise noted, are from the New Revised Standard
Version of the Bible, © 1989 by the Division of Christian Education of the
National Council of Churches of Christ in the United States of America and are
used by permission. Some verses have been altered to reflect greater inclusivity.
The abbreviation NIV is used for the New International Version.

Printed in the United States of America on acid-free paper

09    08    07    06    05          5    4    3    2

Library of Congress Cataloging-in-Publication Data

Geoffrion, Jill Kimberly Hartwell, 1958–
    Christian prayer and labyrinths : pathways to faith, hope, and love /
Jill Kimberly Hartwell Geoffrion.
        p. cm.
    Includes bibliographical references (p.    ).
    ISBN 0-8298-1634-8 (pbk. : alk. paper)
    1. Labyrinths—Religious aspects—Christianity.    2. Spiritual life—
Christianity.    3. Prayer—Christianity.    I. Title.

BV4509.5.G445 2004
248.4'6—dc22                                                    2004053475

# Contents

❦

## PART SIX
### Experiencing Christ in the Labyrinth: Prayers & Poems

## PART SEVEN
### Labyrinth Dedications

## PART EIGHT
### Reflecting on Your Sacred Explorations

## PART NINE
### Learning More

# With Gratitude

I would like to thank the many people who have come to labyrinth events I have facilitated. In honor of their hunger for a deeper connection with God, I have prayed my way to the pages that follow.

I would also like to thank those who shared their gifts in this book, including Cheryl Dudley, who worked with me to create accessible labyrinth introductions for seekers, Robert Ferré for his lovely and accurate image of the Chartres Labyrinth, Lisa Gidlow Moriarty for the beautiful Dancing Woman Labyrinth© pattern, and Elizabeth Nagel for the questions we developed when leading retreats together.

My gratitude also extends to Lauren Artress, Barbara Battin, Linda Campbell, Kate Christianson, Cheryl Dudley, Martha Erickson, Robert Ferré, Tim Geoffrion, Ruth Hanna, Lucy Hartwell, Sarah Henrich, Sally Johnson, Pam Kearney, Mary Kaye Medinger, and Lisa Gidlow Moriarty for their careful attention when the manuscript was still being developed.

Special thanks are also offered to my brother, David Hartwell, and my sister-in-law, Elizabeth Debaut, who shared their peaceful cabin so that I could write without interruption and to my editor, Pamela Johnson, for her commitment to the book, vision, insights, and support.

# Introduction

❧

Incorporating labyrinth praying into my ongoing and ever developing spiritual life has been fruitful. It has led me down pleasant paths of pilgrimage and creativity, into transformative relationships, and labyrinth praying has led me through an extended and very fertile "dark night of the soul." In addition, occasional sojourns into the foreign territory of sacred geometry have led me toward ever deepening expressions of love and joy. Jesus has been my trusted companion on each and every labyrinth encounter. I consider the labyrinth one of the most cherished gifts from God in my life.

The longer I pray the labyrinth, the stronger becomes my urge to share its gifts with others. Writing books is one way in which God has allowed me to do this. I have also had the privilege of leading Christian worship services and retreats where those present used the labyrinth to walk with Christ. Because we have several labyrinths in our yard, and shovel others onto the surface of the frozen lake by our house in the winter, many people have come to pray while experiencing our labyrinths. As I meet with these faithful people, I have witnessed Christ's work through the labyrinth time and time again.

The contemporary revival of labyrinth use continues to grow in both secular and religious communities. Many books, including my own, have been addressed to both secular and religious groups. As an ordained minister whose doctoral study focused in the area of Christian spiritualities, I have longed to offer resources for Christians and Christian faith communities that will initiate or enhance a labyrinth ministry within their own religious context.

In this book you will find many resources for using labyrinths in Christian prayer and ministry. If you are interested in knowing the history of Christian use of labyrinths and if you are wondering about Christian theological considerations relating to labyrinth use, you will find information here. If you are looking for exercises to use personally or for a church event or retreat, they are included. If you need an example of a labyrinth dedication, you will find several in Part Seven. The table of contents will lead you to biblical resources, journal pages, suggestions about preparing for labyrinth encounters, and many other highly usable resources to enhance your labyrinth ministry.

My prayer is that each page of this book will offer you an invitation to pray the labyrinth in ways that support your spiritual maturation. May Christ continue to use labyrinths to help us all journey into the joyous possibilities of faith, hope, and love!

## PART ONE

# INTRODUCING LABYRINTHS

## A QUICK INTRODUCTION TO LABYRINTHS*

What is a labyrinth?
It is a path for prayer
that leads from yearning
towards joy, meaning, hope, and peace.
While it can be used for personal explorations,
it also invites communal participation.
What is planted here flowers in the gardens of our lives.
Whether perplexed, overjoyed, confused, hopeful,
hurt, distraught, happy, or simply curious,
as we pray, God meets us here.
It is not unusual to emerge from the labyrinth inspired,
encouraged, grateful, and clearer about next steps.

*This quick introduction to labyrinths and the suggestions for praying a labyrinth that follow were jointly prepared by Jill K. H. Geoffrion and Cheryl Felicia Dudley. Cheryl's labyrinth ministry, *Soul by Sole*, has grown out of her ministry context in the American Baptist Churches.

## SUGGESTIONS FOR PRAYING A LABYRINTH

Be open as you begin.
Notice what comes.
Welcome God.
Use all that happens, including distractions, as mirrors of your life.
Follow where you are led,
even if you end up moving off "the path."
Tread, leap, stop, sprint, dance, pause, continue on.
Move with the rhythm that suits the moment; it may ebb and flow.
Enjoy the center. Why hurry away?
Let Christ know your heart and mind.
Welcome Jesus' input.
Let any insights or thankfulness
that comes bubble over.

## LABYRINTHS IN CHRISTIAN HISTORY

In 324 C.E. Christians placed a labyrinth on the floor of their church in Algiers, North Africa. Although followers of Christ must have been using the labyrinth earlier, this is the first documented example available. Since that time labyrinths have been prayed, studied, danced, traced, and drawn as Christians have sought to use this spiritual tool in public worship and private prayer.

Although many contemporary churches use the beautiful Chartres labyrinth pattern, historically many different patterns have been used. There is no one "Christian" labyrinth pattern. Labyrinths of various dimensions, materials, colors, and shapes have been utilized by faith communities throughout the ages. Local history, congregational character, and available materials seem to have influenced the choices that different churches made when constructing their labyrinths in or near their places of worship.

Church leaders have made use of labyrinth images in different ways. Using the metaphor of a labyrinth to illustrate important Christian beliefs can be traced as far back as the fourth century when several early church fathers, including Ambrose, Gregory of Nyysa, and Jerome, wrote about labyrinths. Later, beginning in the ninth century, monks working in monastery scriptoriums utilized labyrinth images to illustrate their manuscripts, many of which related to the seasons and the passage of time. Familiarity with the images resulted in many churches, especially those in France, installing large-scale labyrinths on their floors during the twelfth and thirteenth centuries.

There is no uniform historical Christian interpretation of the single-path labyrinth. Theologians of different periods have utilized the pattern to emphasize beliefs that were most relevant to their time. Christ's guidance of believers, the need to follow divine leading, and the importance of moving away from evil towards spiritual maturity are common in church writings and drawings that relate to labyrinths.

Based on legal documents from the Middle Ages it is evident that the clergy working in at least two churches in France used the labyrinth for a dance on Easter afternoon. There are no known surviving historical documents that might shed light on how else the labyrinths were used by the congregations that housed them. The valued presence of labyrinths within churches is sure; we can only hope that more historical information will come to light as researchers continue their work.

## CONTEMPORARY CHRISTIAN USE OF LABYRINTHS

Using a labyrinth for religious purposes involves both moving your body and opening your heart in faith. A "typical" labyrinth experience involves preparing yourself at the threshold, following the single path to the center, spending time in the center, following the same pathway from the center out, crossing the threshold, and then responding to the experience.

"What is the correct way to pray a labyrinth?" is a common question asked by those being introduced to a labyrinth. There is no single "right" way: praying in whatever way helps you connect with God during the labyrinth encounter is the "right" way and serves as the best guide possible!

Praying on the labyrinth is a continuation of your other experiences of prayer; using prayer forms that are familiar is often useful. A few suggestions for praying on the labyrinth include: have a conversation with God about the things that matter most, repeat the words of a favorite prayer, make gestures of praise, recite scriptural phrases such as, "Thy will be done," or present prayer requests to Christ. Another simple way to pray the labyrinth is to pray for others on the pathway in, enjoy God's presence in the center, and pray for oneself while moving on the pathway back towards the threshold. Just as there is no one correct way to pray, there is no single "acceptable" way to pray the labyrinth!

The word "labyrinth" is not found in the Bible, but themes of following God's way, spiritual journeys, and enjoying God's presence—all central to labyrinth experiences—are found throughout Scripture. Many have found that reciting Scripture on the labyrinth focuses their attention on biblical teaching and their relationship to the Divine. For instance, a person may find it helpful to pray, "You show me the path of life. In your presence there is fullness of joy" (Psa. 16:11) or Jesus' words, "I am the way, and the truth, and the life" (John 14:6) while moving on a labyrinth.

During the current period of labyrinth revival, churches, retreat centers, and Christian camps are placing these prayer tools indoors and outdoors. Christians all over the world are installing labyrinths in their yards and gardens. Many are using the labyrinths as ministry tools, bringing portable versions to prisons, national denominational conferences, and church group meetings. It is conservatively estimated that there are more than five thousand labyrinths in the United States alone. God is blessing the use of the labyrinth; many are being drawn closer to Jesus, experiencing healing, and gaining spiritual clarity as they pray on its path.

**CHRISTIAN THEOLOGICAL TOUCHSTONES**

When used from a faith perspective, labyrinths are spiritual tools that help people to perceive and connect with God's presence. The following questions can help you and other Christians experience labyrinths as valuable tools for communing with God.

What biblical verses and concepts support a Christian understanding of labyrinths?

- Labyrinths are spiritual tools that facilitate the various types of prayer illustrated in the Hebrew and Christian Scriptures, including, but not limited to, intercession, praise, meditation, confession, and free-flowing conversation.
- Concepts of journeying in faith and following God's path help link biblical teaching and labyrinth experience.
- Those using labyrinths often report experiences of Christ's inviting, enlightening, and grace-full presence. Biblical themes of love, joy, peace, truth, comfort, guidance, service, and wisdom are particularly relevant to these encounters.

What are some of the Christian theological messages of labyrinths?

- Divine help is available. A path of wisdom leads one towards God.
- Religious devotion can be intensely pleasurable.
- Truth and God's presence are yoked. As one moves in the Divine Presence, truth becomes clearer and more compelling.

- Moving one's body in faith can support one's desire for spiritual connection.
- Journeying towards intimacy with God is seldom a linear process.
- Sacred patterns can assist seekers in moving beyond their own limitations. God speaks through visual symbols.
- Love for God leads to personal encounters with the Divine, and to a commitment to acting in faith.
- Desire for wider service springs naturally from time spent with God.

What can be learned about God by using labyrinths?

- God is real—and accessible.
- God values truth and communicates it freely.
- God's presence supports wholeness.
- God is unpredictable—but trustworthy. We cannot control or even anticipate God's next move in our lives.

What about Jesus and the labyrinth?

Labyrinths were in use long before the time of Jesus. We have no record of Jesus referring to or using a labyrinth, although the decorative Greek key pattern was well known and used in Palestine during Jesus' lifetime. This simple pattern can be extended to the shape of a seven-circuit "classical" labyrinth.

Early in the first century Christians began using the labyrinth in the practice of their faith. As early as 324 C.E. labyrinths were being placed in churches. Historically they have been used as a way to symbolize and connect with the risen Christ's presence, power, and love.

There is a revival of labyrinth interest among contemporary Christians. They use the labyrinth to deepen their faith in Jesus, to encounter Christ's presence, and to be strengthened by God to live out their calling to follow Jesus.

## PART TWO

# BECOMING FAMILIAR WITH LABYRINTHS

*If you want to know God better, take a walk with God.*
—Four-year-old Asa

## IF YOU HAVEN'T EXPERIENCED A LABYRINTH BEFORE

The labyrinth is easy to use. Here's all that you need to know:

There is just one path that leads to and from the center in a labyrinth. You cross the threshold, follow the path in to the center, enjoy your experience there for as long as you like, and take the same path back out across the threshold. This is not a maze—there are no dead ends in a labyrinth, only turning points that lead one closer to the center.

Feel free to walk around other people if their pace is different or if they stop. It's okay for other people to move around you. If you feel "tippy" or dizzy, it may be helpful to slow down, speed up, or focus on a point in the distance. Some find it helpful to stop at each turn. The path can be a two-way street. Do what comes naturally when you meet someone else, just as you would if you were walking on a narrow sidewalk.

Take advantage of this opportunity to pray with your whole body. Give yourself permission to follow the intuitions and desires that come. Remember that this is designed to be an embodied prayer experience. Be open to your body expressing itself through gestures, movements, or the flow of tears. Don't be trapped by the thought, "I can't do *that*, other people are watching!" Other people are busy with their own labyrinth experiences.

You can't get lost on a labyrinth, but you can get turned around. If you move off the path and forget which way you were heading, step back on and begin moving. You will either end up at the threshold or the center. From there you can decide to continue or end your experience.

You may choose to walk the path from the threshold to the center and from the center back out, or to explore the labyrinth pattern in another way. For instance, you may wish to walk around the labyrinth, experience it by witnessing others as they move on it, sit beside it—the possibilities are limitless. If an idea comes, try it! There are as many ways to pray labyrinths as there are people who use them.

Many have experienced the labyrinth as a mirror where it is possible to view one's life internally and externally at the same time. Open your heart; open your mind to what you may notice. Be compassionate with yourself; judging yourself isn't helpful.

Labyrinth experiences are seldom "done" when one leaves the pattern. You may wish to journal, walk around the labyrinth, use art supplies to explore the meanings of your time on the labyrinth, or sit quietly to let what has begun continue to grow. You may not become aware of all the meanings of your labyrinth encounter for hours, days, or even months.

Witnessing others as they move in prayer can be a very meaningful way of readying yourself for your prayer on a labyrinth. One of the many gifts the labyrinth offers us is being in a place where we can practice watching others with eyes of prayer rather than eyes of judgment.

Before you enter, let go of any expectations about what may happen during your labyrinth experience. Pay attention to whatever develops as you move in prayer. Be open to what is happening as it occurs. Try to let go of thoughts that distract you from being present to the experience.

It is often helpful to respond to your labyrinth experience by writing, drawing, or using some other creative process.

People of faith have been walking this prayer path for centuries. Now it is your turn . . .

## A SUGGESTED PROCESS FOR PRAYING THE LABYRINTH

Take time to gather yourself before entering the labyrinth; this may include a mental prayer or a body gesture like bowing or crossing yourself. After traversing the threshold follow the pathway toward the center. Enter the center, taking as much time as you need there. Stand, sit, kneel, or lie down if you would like. When you are ready, follow the pathway out. Be conscious of crossing the threshold between the labyrinth and whatever lies beyond it. Before leaving the experience, take time to express gratitude. Whenever possible, revisit your experience in a way that will be useful to you whether through journaling, drawing, silent meditation, dancing, singing, or mental consideration. Mine the riches of your labyrinth encounter using whatever means are most helpful.

The labyrinth is a safe space. If for any reason you do not want to continue, you can leave the pattern at any time. Relax. Enjoy.

## PRAYING LABYRINTHS WITH YOUR FINGERS OR EYES

Labyrinths can be experienced in many different ways. Pray the following patterns with colored markers, your fingers, your eyes, or in any other ways that come to heart and mind. Notice how your entire body responds to these prayers.

**The Chartres Labyrinth**

Use your finger, a pen, or your eyes
to follow the labyrinth's pathway to the center and back out.

*The Chartres Labyrinth was constructed
around 1201 C.E. This geometrically accurate
rendition of the floor labyrinth was drawn by
Robert Ferré.*

### A Seven-Circuit "Classical" Labyrinth

Use your finger, a pen, or your eyes
to follow the labyrinth's pathway to the center and back out.

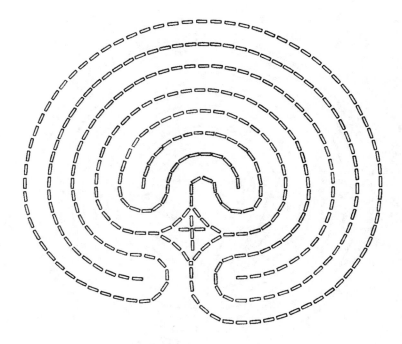

*This diagram was drawn by*
*Lisa Gidlow Moriarty.*

## The Heart of Chartres Labyrinth

Use your finger, a pen, or your eyes
to follow the labyrinth's pathway to the center and back out.

*The Heart of Chartres pattern is derived from the
five inner rings and the center of the labyrinth found on
the floor of Chartres Cathedral in France. This diagram
was drawn by Lisa Gidlow Moriarty and was adapted
from an original drawing by Robert Ferré.*

## A Four-Circuit Labyrinth with Spiral Center

Use your finger, a pen, or your eyes
to follow the labyrinth's pathway to the center and back out.

*This diagram was drawn by
Lisa Gidlow Moriarty.*

**The Dancing Woman Labyrinth©**

Use your finger, a pen, or your eyes
to follow the labyrinth's pathways.

*This diagram was drawn by*
*Lisa Gidlow Moriarty.*
*Lisa created this original pattern.*

## A Three-Circuit Labyrinth

Use your finger, a pen, or your eyes
to follow the labyrinth's pathway to the center and back out.

*This diagram was drawn by
Lisa Gidlow Moriarty.*

## PART THREE

# INDIVIDUAL LABYRINTH PRAYING

The resources in this section are designed
to help individuals enjoy the labyrinth in a variety
of meaningful ways. The exercises may be easily
adapted for use with groups.

## WHY I PRAY THE LABYRINTH

Given all the ways to pray, why do I choose to use labyrinths so frequently? The joy, gratitude, deep spiritual knowing, beauty, creativity, love,
and experience of Jesus' presence I experience there all call me to the path.

I am amazed by the pleasure of labyrinth praying. Many, but certainly
not all, experiences of praying the labyrinth are joyful. I have wept pro-
foundly as I poured out my pain to God on the path. However, the
labyrinth doesn't seem to be a place where my prayer gets lost in sorrow,
details, or holding on to preconceived notions of what I want or need. As
I move along the path, whether with my feet, my eyes, my knees, or my
fingers, I am often aware of God's compassionate presence with me. That
is the essence of my pleasure, something I am always ready to experience!

"Thank You!" is the prayer phrase that I find myself using most often
as I move on labyrinths. Springing from the soil of my labyrinth encounters, it is my deepest and most spontaneous message to God. Oddly
enough, this "Thank You" is not something I set out to communicate. I am
not aware of it being for anything specific. Yet time and time again I find
myself on the labyrinth filled with profound gratitude.

Silence and stillness powerfully call to me. Unfortunately, my desire
to pray meditatively and my ability to pray quietly without moving are not
equally matched. Yet as I engage the labyrinth pattern with my body, I am
able to enter the deeper realms of spiritual connection almost effortlessly.
We do not expect the delights of faith to be accessed so easily; when using
labyrinths they often are.

At times structure aids my praying. Sometimes I need spontaneity to
lead me towards God. The labyrinth can support both structure and
spontaneity. When structure is called for, the path with its singular route
to and from the center awaits. Yet I never feel bound to use the labyrinth
in only one prescribed way. When grieving for my father-in-law, who had
died suddenly, I moved directly to the center and sat there until I was
ready to get up and move directly out. Sometimes I walk around and
around the labyrinth, or just sit near it as I commune with the Holy
Spirit. I feel drawn to know God and be known by God in increasingly

profound ways when I am in the presence of a labyrinth. What could be more meaningful?

Should prayer be beautiful? My artist's heart beats faster at the possibility. My awe of labyrinths as spiritual tools includes deep appreciation for the ways in which they allow beauty and praying to come together. The sacred possibilities of beauty are not only visible when looking at labyrinth patterns, they are also visceral when encountering them.

The centering effect of labyrinth praying aids me in opening my mind and heart to the day's best possibilities. That's why I often pray a labyrinth before beginning my workday. As a retreat leader and spiritual guide I have come to trust labyrinths as spiritual prayer tools. I am not surprised by the ways in which labyrinths open the floodgates of creativity in those who use them, but I am continually amazed by the magnitude of the creative energy that is unleashed by their use. It is nothing less than astounding!

Jesus' presence with me on the labyrinth has comforted, surprised, challenged, and supported me. Like Jesus' disciples on the road to Emmaus (Luke 24:13–32), my heart often burns within me as I walk a labyrinth with the risen Christ, pouring out my heart, and listening to the wisdom that is given through God's Spirit. Although there is no mention of a labyrinth in the Bible, the scriptural image of Jesus being the Way has taken on a fuller meaning as I have come to know the labyrinth pathway more intimately.

Whatever your need, I hope that you too will pray the labyrinth and experience all the wonderful surprises and gifts God has for you there.

## WELCOME TO THE LABYRINTH

You're here!
This is the well
you have been seeking.

Put down your luggage anywhere;
it will be attended to.

That distinctive scent is from a burning candle.
Love lit it—in anticipation of your arrival.

Beauty will help you get oriented.
She usually suggests,
"Leave your shoes by the front door."

Please make yourself at home.


## SUGGESTED APPROACHES FOR PRAYERFUL LABYRINTH ENCOUNTERS

There are at least as many ways to pray a labyrinth as there are people who pray it. The following suggestions pair a spiritual activity such as discerning or praising with a phrase or an idea that can help you pray on the labyrinth.

CARING     "God, [person's name] is in need . . ."

CENTERING     As you feel or perceive God's presence, move into it more deeply.

CHANTING     Sing "Kyrie eleison," "Alleluia," or a favorite Taizé chant.

DISCERNING     Ask God for input about something important.

FOCUSING     Repeat a favorite name for God, such as, "Jesus, Jesus . . ." or, "Healer, Healer . . ."

Say a spiritual word that has significance for you, perhaps, "Love, love, love . . ."

Utter a short prayer, such as "Please help!" "Thy will be done," or "I'm available."

| | |
|---|---|
| GRIEVING | "Please help me to stay present to this pain. Support me as I move with it." |
| IMAGING | Hold someone or something in an internal visual state that represents your deepest desire. |
| INTERCEDING | Plead with God on behalf of others. |
| MOVING | Embody your sacred communication. No words are necessary. |
| OPENING | "I'm here. Help me to stay open to all You wish to communicate." |
| PRAISING | Speak God's name or attributes with love and appreciation. |
| QUESTIONING | "What is my next step?" |
| | "What do I need?" |
| | "What is changing?" |
| READING AND REFLECTING | Read or recall a biblical story. Ponder its meanings as you move. Take your scriptures with you. Stop anywhere to read and respond. |
| RELEASING | "Help me let go of . . ." |
| | "I forgive . . ." |
| SEARCHING | "God, I want to understand . . ." |
| SEEKING | "God, reveal Yourself to me." |
| SINGING | Choose a favorite spiritual song, or hymn. Sing or hum it silently or out loud. Set your pace to the cadence of the tune. |
| TRANSITIONING | "Ever since [person's name] died . . ." |
| | "Thank You, God, for the new opportunity . . ." |

## LABYRINTH PRAYING FOR CHANGE

*Do not remember the former things, or consider the things of old. I am about to do a new thing; now it springs forth, do you not perceive it? I will make a way in the wilderness and rivers in the desert.* —Isaiah 43:18–19

Begin by finding a place on the labyrinth where you would like to be. Stand or sit in a comfortable position; you will be here for several minutes.

Close your eyes. Starting with your exhalation, take three deep breaths. Open your eyes and read Isaiah 43:18–19 silently or out loud. In silence pray about what these verses are coming to mean for you. Take at least five minutes to do so.

Now walk the labyrinth three different times, considering the possible meanings of these verses.

On your first walk consider how you and God are moving towards new things. On your second walk focus on how you and your community of faith are being invited by God to new things. On your third walk pray and reflect on how our larger society and world community is being invited by God towards new things. You may make these three walks in any order that makes sense to you. Resist any temptation to complete only one or two of the walks. You are strongly encouraged to complete all three; each will yield a different harvest.

When you are finished, take time to reflect on your experiences. If it would be helpful, reflect while circling around the outside of the labyrinth. You may want to journal or respond with art supplies after each of your three experiences.

If you would like to return to the labyrinth to deepen this exploration, use one or more of these biblical verses to focus your prayer.

- "You shall have to clear out the old to make way for the new" (Lev. 26:10b).
- "God's mercies never come to an end; they are new every morning; great is your faithfulness" (Lam. 3:22b–23).
- "A new heart I will give you, and a new spirit I will put within you; and I will remove from your body the heart of stone and give you a heart of flesh." (Ezek. 36:26).

- "I [ Jesus] give you a new commandment, that you love one another. Just as I have loved you, you also should love one another" ( John 13:34).

## PRAYING GOD'S NAME ON THE LABYRINTH

Select one of the biblical names for God from the list below, or identify a name for the Divine that has particular significance to you. Repeat it with loving devotion as you walk the labyrinth.

### Hebrew Testament

| | |
|---|---|
| The One who sees me | *Genesis 16:13* |
| Mighty One | *Psalm 50:1* |
| The One of Sinai | *Judges 5:5* |
| Holy One | *Job 6:10; Psalm 22:3* |
| Righteous One | *Proverbs 21:12* |

### Christian Testament

| | |
|---|---|
| Blessed One | *Mark 14:61* |
| The Chosen One | *Luke 23:35* |
| The One who calls you | *Galatians 5:8* |
| Living One | *Revelation 1:18* |
| The One who is and was | *Revelation 11:17* |

## BIBLICAL PHRASES TO USE WHILE PRAYING THE LABYRINTH

Sometimes it is helpful to use a scriptural phrase to focus your prayer on the labyrinth. Pick one or more of the verses listed below and let it orient your praying as you move.

- "My hope is from God" (Psa. 62:5b).
- "In the day of my trouble I call on you, for you will answer me" (Psa. 86: 7).
- "God is merciful and gracious, slow to anger and abounding in steadfast love" (Psa. 103:8).
- "God restores my soul" (Psa. 23:3a).

- "Worship God with gladness; come into God's presence with singing" (Psa. 100:2).

- "My soul clings to you; your right hand upholds me" (Psa. 63:8).

- "I will remember your miracles of long ago" (Psa. 77:11b NIV).

- "God is the strength of my heart" (Psa. 73:26b).

- "O God, you have searched me and known me" (Psa. 139:1).

- "Take delight in God, and God will give you the desires of your heart" (Psa. 37:4).

- "I praise you [God], for I am fearfully and wonderfully made" (Psa. 139:14a).

- "Lead me in the way everlasting" (Psa. 139:24b).

- "There is surely a future hope for you, and our hope will not be cut off" (Prov. 23:18 NIV).

- "God gives power to the faint, and strengthens the powerless" (Isa. 40:29).

- "O God, hear; O God, forgive; O God, listen and act and do not delay!" (Dan. 9:19).

- "Where two or three are gathered in my [Jesus'] name, I am there among them" (Matt. 18:20).

- "I [Jesus] am with you always, to the end of the age" (Matt. 28:20b).

- "The truth will make you free" (John 8:32).

- "My peace I to give you" (Jesus quoted in John 14:27b).

- "God's love has been poured into our hearts by the Holy Spirit that has been given to us" (Rom. 5:5).

- "God is a refuge of the oppressed, a stronghold in times of trouble" (Psa. 9:9).

- "And now faith, hope, and love abide, these three; and the greatest of these is love" (1 Cor. 13:13).

- "We do not lose heart. Even though our outer nature is wasting away, our inner nature is being renewed day by day" (2 Cor. 4:16).

- "My [Christ's] grace is sufficient for you, for power is made perfect in weakness" (2 Cor. 12:9b).

- "Cast all your anxiety on God, because God cares for you" (1 Pet. 5:7).

- "If my father and mother forsake me, God will take me up" (Psa. 27:10).

## PART FOUR

# GROUP LABYRINTH PRAYING

*Praying the labyrinth with others can be a
true delight. Sharing the sacred space while being
present to one's own experience provides opportunities
for growth and nurture in community.
These exercises can be adapted for individuals.*

## A CIRCLE OF PRAISE AROUND THE LABYRINTH

This simple prayer exercise can be used at the beginning of any labyrinth event.

Form a circle around or on the labyrinth. If you have a large group, circle the outside of the labyrinth. For a smaller group, form a circle around the center of the labyrinth. If group members would be comfortable doing so, invite everyone to join hands.

The leader offers words of focus, such as, "We are standing around a simple yet profound pattern of God's love. As we let the symbol and its messages of faith in, let us become aware of the community of Christ-followers that we are, and let us offer silent or verbal words of praise to God."

The leader becomes silent and waits for group members to respond.

When it seems that the flow of praise is coming to an end, but not before one full minute has passed, the leader says, "Amen."

Participants are then invited to move to the next setting and activity of the event.

## WORSHIPPING ON THE LABYRINTH USING PSALM 103

After a brief labyrinth introduction, the leader explains that the labyrinth will be used as a place of communal praise for the next thirty-five to forty minutes. Participants are encouraged to enter the labyrinth as they feel ready and to walk it at their own pace. If they exit the labyrinth before the leader is finished, they are invited to walk around the circumference of the labyrinth, sit quietly by the labyrinth, or use art supplies as a way of continuing their prayerful praise.

Each five minutes the leader will read one of the following verses from Psalm 103. Those walking the labyrinth will be invited to praise God in response. Depending on the nature of the group, people can be encouraged to offer their prayers of praise silently or verbally.

As people begin entering the labyrinth, read Psalm 103:1, "Bless God, O my soul, and all that is within me, bless God's holy name." The leader adds, "Let us praise God." (The people offer their prayers of praise silently or verbally after each verse of the psalm is read.)

Five minutes later read Psalm 103:6, "God works vindication and justice for all who are oppressed." The leader adds, "Let us praise God."

Five minutes later read Psalm 103:8, "God is merciful and gracious, slow to anger and abounding in steadfast love." The leader adds, "Let us praise God."

Five minutes later read Psalm 103:12, "As far as the east is from the west, so far God removes our transgressions from us." The leader adds, "Let us praise God."

Five minutes later read Psalm 103:17, "The steadfast love of God is from everlasting to everlasting on those who fear God, and God's righteousness to children's children." The leader adds, "Let us praise God."

Five minutes later read Psalm 103:22b, "Bless God, O my soul." The leader adds, "Let us praise God."

Five minutes later read the entire Psalm 103:1–22:

Bless God, O my soul, and all that is within me, bless God's holy name. Bless God, O my soul, and do not forget all God's benefits—who forgives all your iniquity, who heals all your diseases, who redeems your life from the Pit, who crowns you with steadfast love and mercy, who satisfies you with good as long as you live so that your youth is renewed like the eagle's.

God works vindication and justice for all who are oppressed. God made known God's ways to Moses, God's acts to the people of Israel. God is merciful and gracious, slow to anger and abounding in steadfast love. God will not always accuse, nor will God keep God's anger forever. God does not deal with us according to our sins, nor repay us according to our iniquities. For as the heavens are high above the earth, so great is God's steadfast love toward those who fear God; as far as the east is from the west, so far God removes our transgressions from us. As a father has compassion for his children, so God has compassion for those who fear God. For God knows how we were made; God remembers that we are dust.

As for mortals, their days are like grass; they flourish like a flower of the field; for the wind passes over it, and it is gone, and its place knows it no more. But the steadfast love of God is from everlasting to everlasting on those who fear God, and God's righteousness to children's children, to those who keep God's covenant and remember to do God's commandments.

God has established God's throne in the heavens, and God's kingdom rules over all. Bless God, O God's angels, you mighty ones who do his bidding, obedient to God's spoken word. Bless God, all God's hosts, God's ministers that do God's will. Bless God, all God's works, in all places of God's dominion. Bless God, O my soul.

The leader adds, "Let us praise God."

When it seems that the prayers of the group are coming to an end, the leader says, "Praise God! Amen."

## LABYRINTH SWEEPING: PRAYING TOWARDS FORGIVENESS*

This labyrinth experience requires a broom. Each person in the group is invited to take a broom with him or her to the labyrinth.

Ask each person in the group to silently identify someone (it could be him- or herself) that that person needs to forgive. Each person should be specific about whom he or she is forgiving and what he or she is forgiving them for.

It may help individuals in the group to sweep around the labyrinth as they prepare themselves. People may sweep clockwise or counterclockwise, whichever feels right—or both! This is each person's opportunity to seek divine help in doing what is difficult, to forgive.

Ask each person to sweep and pray "in" those things that will help in forgiving (such as graciousness, understanding, kindness), or sweep "out" those things that stand in the way of forgiveness. Each person can decide if the need to forgive would best be supported by a sweeping "in" movement or a sweeping "out" movement, or both. All can use the labyrinth path to pray as they sweep. They can sweep in towards the center, go directly to the center and sweep out from there, or sweep their way in and then out.

As each person finishes sweeping, ask each one to take time to reflect on the meanings of the experience. Many people find it helpful to write their thoughts out or work with art supplies as they continue their explorations.

*This exercise was inspired by an e-mail from Bev Hof-Miller to the Labyrinth Society Energy Keepers in which she described "Sweeping in the New Year" on a labyrinth.

# PART FIVE

## GUIDED LABYRINTH PRAYING
### Scriptures, Questions, and Prayers

*Bible verses to ponder and pray are offered on the following pages.
You may wish to explore these verses personally or with a group. A question
and a prayer follow each scripture. Use the space after the question to explore your
thoughts. As other verses, questions, and prayers come to mind and heart,
let them lead you. You may close your labyrinth experience with the prayer
provided or another one that flows from your reflection.*

**PROVERBS 23:19**

"Hear, my child, and be wise, and direct your mind in the way."

On a labyrinth, how do my mind and body work together as they orient me towards God?

Christ, as I use the labyrinth, guide my mind towards spiritual maturity.

**PSALM 16:11**

"You show me the path of life.
In your presence there is fullness of joy;
in your right hand are pleasures forevermore."

How is the labyrinth a "path of life" for me?

Christ, what paths of life are You revealing to me as I pray the labyrinth?

**2 JOHN 1:6**

"This is love, that we walk according to God's commandments; this is the commandment just as you have heard it from the beginning—you must walk in it."

In what ways is the fruit of my labyrinth praying perceptible to others?

Christ, love me. May our love be the fuel of my loving actions.

**PSALM 23:3**

"God restores my soul.
God leads me in right paths for God's name's sake."

Why might I have been led to the path known as the labyrinth?

Christ, thank You for leading me on the labyrinth path. May my involvement with the labyrinth glorify You.

**PSALM 119:105**

"Your word is a lamp to my feet and a light to my path."

What is God communicating to me as I use the labyrinth today?

Christ, thank You for Your faithful guidance.

**MICAH 6:8**

"He has told you, O mortal, what is good;
  and what does God require of you but to do justice,
  and to love kindness, and to walk humbly with your God?"

By observing others experiencing the labyrinth, what can I learn about walking humbly with God?

Christ, teach me through others to do justice, act in kindness, and walk humbly in faith.

## JOHN 14:6

"Jesus said . . . 'I am the way, and the truth, and the life.'"

If Jesus appeared to me on the labyrinth and said, "I am the way, and the truth, and the life," how would I respond?

Christ, be my way, my truth, and my life.

**PSALM 18:36**

"You gave me a wide place for my steps under me,
and my feet did not slip."

In what ways do I experience the labyrinth as a safe place to pray?

Christ, thank You for making a way for me and for helping me not to stumble.

**DEUTERONOMY 11:18–19 (NIV)**

"Fix these words of mine [God's] in your hearts and minds; tie them as symbols on your hands and bind them on your foreheads. Teach them to your children, talking about them when you sit at home and when you walk along the road, when you lie down and when you get up."

What spiritual conversations might I have with family members while using a labyrinth?

Christ, may my words be Your words—on the labyrinth and elsewhere.

**ISAIAH 30:21**

"And when you turn to the right or when you turn to the left,
your ears shall hear a word behind you, saying,
'This is the way; walk in it.'"

How willing am I to trust a winding way to lead me where I need to go?

Christ, help me to trust You and Your way, even when it seems like I'm going in circles and getting nowhere.

## LEVITICUS 26:12

"I will walk among you, and will be your God,
and you shall be my people."

In what ways do I perceive God's walking with me on the labyrinth?

Christ, as You walk among us, allow us the grace to know You better.

**JEREMIAH 6:16**

"Thus says God: Stand at the crossroads, and look,
and ask for the ancient paths, where the good way lies;
and walk in it, and find rest for your souls.

What paths has God revealed to me during the crossroad times of my life?
Am I walking in the good way?

Christ, help me to choose to walk on the paths that lead to life.

**ISAIAH 52:7**

"How beautiful upon the mountains are the feet of the messenger who announces peace, who brings good news, who announces salvation, who says to Zion, 'Your God reigns.'"

What words of praise to God might someone utter while watching my feet moving on a labyrinth?

Christ, what good news, messages of peace, and announcements of salvation would You like me to share?

**PROVERBS 4:18**

"But the path of the righteous is like the light of dawn,
which shines brighter and brighter until full day."

How is my service to God in the community nourished by my ongoing use of labyrinths?

Christ, may Your light shine brightly through me.

**PSALM 25:4**

"Make me to know your ways, O God; teach me your paths."

Why is it important that I experience the labyrinth path with my body and my mind?

Christ, I'm here, open, and available.

**3 JOHN 1:3**

"I was overjoyed when some of the friends arrived and testified to your faithfulness to the truth, namely how you walk in the truth."

Why might my labyrinth experiences be called, "Walking in the truth"?

Christ, help me to walk in truth; help me to be true.

**NEHEMIAH 9:19**

"You [God] in your great mercies did not forsake [the Israelites] in the wilderness; the pillar of cloud that led them in the way did not leave them by day, nor the pillar of fire by night that gave them light on the way by which they should go."

What is God's presence on the labyrinth teaching me about "the way I should go"?

Christ, I give to You my fears of being forsaken and abandoned.

## ISAIAH 40:14

"Whom did God consult for enlightenment,
and who taught God the path of justice?"

In what ways does my experience with labyrinths challenge and support me in following paths of justice?

Christ, grant me the clarity and courage to choose a path of justice.

**PSALM 119:45 (NIV)**

"I will walk about in freedom, for I have sought out your precepts."

What freedoms has God ushered into my life through my use of labyrinths?

Christ, I'm so grateful for the freedom I walk in. Thank You for leading me here.

## PART SIX

EXPERIENCING CHRIST
IN THE LABYRINTH
Prayers and Poems

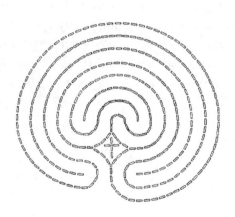

*Experiencing the center of the labyrinth is the heart of one's labyrinth experience both physically and metaphorically. Praying in the center of a labyrinth often inspires creative expressions of faith. These prayers and poems express a taste of the joy, love, and hope that has been offered to me by Christ in the center of many different labyrinths.*

**POWER**

Power,

My life is well held
in Your sure hands.

Amen.

## THE CENTER

I come here every day
in my imagination—
with my breath
and my heart.

So to sit here within you
overwhelms me.
Gratitude spills in every direction.

**HONESTLY**

God,
I am not what I pretend to be.
I am hardly the characters whose costumes I put on
and take off with glee.
I am less than my tears
and more than my laughter.
I am not my projections
or my rejections.
I am not the rivers
which propel my body
or the eddies where in desperation
I gasp for breath.
I am not the strong silent Center
even when I am there.

## THE SAME OLD STORY OF FAITH

God,
I come—
this is my story.

I come—
because I am made to come.

I come—
there is nowhere else I can go.

I come—
carried along in the current.

I come—
this is mystery.

Coming is the most ancient
of all stories.

Perhaps there is no other story.

Where else
is there to go?

## CHRIST OF EARTH,
## CHRIST OF SKY

How very whole it feels
to be drawn downward
by the grass under my feet.

How very integrated it feels
to be pulled upward
by the celestial energy above my head.

You seem to twirl
around me.

Is that You
welling up
within me?

## MORNING PRAYER ON THE LABYRINTH

Christ, *Holy God –*

I feel You
in the warmth of the sun.

I feel You
in the coolness of the wind.

I feel You
in the moistness of the dew.

I feel You
in the firmness of the ground.

I sense You
in the interior silence.

I call to You
from a wordless place of knowing.

I rest
with You.

**BEING HERE**

Christ,

This labyrinth
is
a place
of longing
for You,

a place
of remembrance,
the fuel of hope,

a place
of yearning
for union.


Thank You
for being
in this place
with me.

Thank You
for the softness
that supports me
and the warmth
that caresses me
as I am with You here.

## MY NEST

This labyrinth,
O Christ,
is my nest.

The place
I wait for You
to come
and feed me,

to protect me,

to push me out
so that I may fly.

What a lovely nest—
so safe,
so secure.

Thank You
for being with me
here.

## AFTER SPENDING TIME WITH LABYRINTHS

Christ,
Why have labyrinths captured my imagination, my body, my spirit?
I truly do not understand!
It feels so right to be here—so natural.
And yet sometimes I feel so scared.

Why such strong attraction? Why such passion?
I speak of my relationship with labyrinths as one who is smitten!
Why such commitment to sharing these pathways with others?
Where does the incredible draw to the labyrinth originate?

Why do I ask these questions?
What are my greatest fears?

I fear Truth that changes reality as I have perceived it.

I fear the depth of spiritual connection and openness to God
that I know can happen on a labyrinth.

Yet I am at rest with You within the center of the sacred circle
hopefully and tentatively,
sensing fear and confidence,
grateful yet unsure,
longingly wondering.

Where else can I be with You
with this level of intimacy?

## TRANSFORMATION IN THE LABYRINTH

Invited by You, God, I have come.
What is the gift I offer?

Into Your steady hands of love
I carefully place my brokenness.

Jesus,
I open my heart to Your suffering.

Fearful, yet hopeful
I stand at Your mouth, Consuming Spirit.

Asking that You receive me
as the body of Christ—
digest me,
purify me,
and make me useful.

Transform me into divine energy,
embodying who I was created to become.

May it be so!

# PART SEVEN

## LABYRINTH DEDICATIONS

Each labyrinth has its own dimensions, character, and mission.
The following dedication rituals reflect the unique purpose of each of the
labyrinths for which they were created. As you dedicate a labyrinth in your
yard, church, or community setting, I invite you to adapt these rituals.
May the dedication you create reflect the unique form and function
of the labyrinth that graces your setting.

## DEDICATION OF A PERSONAL CANVAS LABYRINTH
## DURING A GATHERING OF FAMILY AND FRIENDS

CARETAKER OF THE LABYRINTH:
We invite you to bless this particular labyrinth for all the ministries that lie ahead. Let us use as our refrain, "Blessed be God, blessed be God, blessed be God forever."

ALL:
**Blessed be God, blessed be God, blessed be God forever.**

CARETAKER OF THE LABYRINTH:
Please join hands and walk around the labyrinth counterclockwise while paying silent attention to the dreams and possibilities that you hold for this labyrinth.

*(The group circles the labyrinth once.)*

CARETAKER OF THE LABYRINTH:
Let us bless God, who will use this labyrinth in the lives of those who experience it.

ALL:
**Blessed be God, blessed be God, blessed be God forever.**

CARETAKER OF THE LABYRINTH:
Please join hands and walk clockwise around the labyrinth while offering spoken prayers for this beautiful spiritual tool and the ways in which it will be used.

ALL:
**(Spontaneous prayers.)**

*(The group circles the labyrinth once.)*

CARETAKER OF THE LABYRINTH:
Let us bless God, whose love, truth, and beauty will be communicated to those who walk on this canvas.

**ALL:**
**Blessed be God, blessed be God, blessed be God forever.**

CARETAKER OF THE LABYRINTH:
Amen.

## DEDICATION OF A CHARTRES-STYLE PERMANENT LABYRINTH IN A CONGREGATIONAL SETTING

Members of the Labyrinth Stewardship Committee took turns leading this dedication service; therefore, the voices are listed as Stewards One through Five.

STEWARD ONE:
The Chartres-style labyrinth that we have gathered to dedicate includes many Christian messages. The most obvious is centrality of the cross in the design. As you can see, the equal-armed cross spans the entire width of the pattern.

As a sign of respect for the cross, and our unity of Christian purpose, let us each find a place on the labyrinth cross and, while holding hands in two lines that intersect in the center, stand there as we pray.

(Steward walks to a spot on the "cross" and waits for everyone else to do the same. All join hands.)

STEWARD TWO:
We are standing not only on a labyrinth, but also on the materialization of many dreams and prayers for a labyrinth ministry through which many might encounter God's help and grace.

STEWARD THREE:

In the early thirteenth century C.E. a labyrinth in this unique form was laid in the floor of Chartres Cathedral in France. At that time, Christian theologians were very interested in the concept of the New Jerusalem and incorporated many symbols of it in their plans for Chartres Cathedral and its labyrinth. Our dedication for this Chartres-style labyrinth honors this history and connects us to it as we pray using the promises and blessings associated with the New Jerusalem as it is described in the book of Revelation.

STEWARD FOUR:

The congregational response to our prayers will be, "We dedicate this labyrinth to Your glory and the spiritual wholeness of all who come." Please repeat it with me.

ALL:

**We dedicate this labyrinth to Your glory and the spiritual wholeness of all who come.**

STEWARD FOUR:

We read in Revelation 21:3 (NIV), "Now the dwelling of God is with humanity." We pray that those who use this labyrinth will experience Your presence, O Christ.

ALL:

**We dedicate this labyrinth to Your glory and the spiritual wholeness of all who come.**

STEWARD FOUR:

We read in Revelation 21:4 that Christ "will wipe every tear from their eyes." Christ, we ask that all those who come to the labyrinth in pain will receive what is needed from You.

ALL:

**We dedicate this labyrinth to Your glory and the spiritual wholeness of all who come.**

STEWARD FOUR:

In Revelation 21:5 Christ declares, "I am making all things new." For the courage to pray for fresh starts, we ask Your grace, O Christ.

ALL:

**We dedicate this labyrinth to Your glory and the spiritual wholeness of all who come.**

STEWARD FOUR:

In Revelation 21:6 Christ states, "I am the Alpha and Omega, the beginning and end." Christ, may this labyrinth path, where the beginning is also the end, teach us to see, think, and feel the unity of all You have created and all You are."

ALL:

**We dedicate this labyrinth to Your glory and the spiritual wholeness of all who come.**

STEWARD FOUR:

In Revelation 21:6 Christ also promises, "To the one who is thirsty I will give drink without cost from the spring of the water of life." Christ, may all who come to this labyrinth be satisfied by meeting with You here.

ALL:

**We dedicate this labyrinth to Your glory and the spiritual wholeness of all who come.**

STEWARD FOUR:

In Revelation 21:23 (NIV) we read, "The city does not need the sun or the moon to shine on it, for the glory of God gives it light and the Lamb is its lamp." Christ, may those who experience this labyrinth be illumined by Your presence. May Your light shine in them and through them.

ALL:

**We dedicate this labyrinth to Your glory and the spiritual wholeness of all who come.**

STEWARD FOUR:
We offer these prayers in Your name, Jesus. Amen.

STEWARD FIVE:
We are now invited to move from our cross formation and to bless the labyrinth in a different way. For the next hour there will be musicians playing by the labyrinth. When you feel ready, please enter and walk the labyrinth. Today, if you feel led, please pray for all who will be coming to use the labyrinth at our church.

There are art supplies and paper on the table by the threshold of the labyrinth. If you wish to create a visual blessing for our labyrinth, please do so. Any artwork that is left on the table will be displayed.

## DEDICATION OF A PERMANENT OUTDOOR LABYRINTH IN A HOME SETTING

Form a loose circle with all standing on the labyrinth. Invite all to extend the energy that is in their hearts and minds through their hands, palms down, toward the labyrinth.

The communal response for all who are able will be to place both hands on the labyrinth and pray, "We dedicate this labyrinth to spiritual awakening and reawakening."

LEADER:

Each person is invited to call forth the image of a loved one walking this labyrinth, receiving what is needed. (Pause.) Now all are invited to imagine someone for whom it feels difficult, if not impossible, for you to like or accept. Imagine that person walking this labyrinth, receiving what is needed. (Pause.)

COMMUNITY:

**We dedicate this labyrinth to spiritual awakening and reawakening.**

LEADER:

With hearts extending in many directions, Let us pray.

Sacred Sustainer, Way to wholeness, Creator of possibilities, Supporter of change, Forgiving Releaser, Freedom, Honesty, Wisdom, Hope, Joy . . . we thank You for the beautiful spiritual tool on which we are standing. It is our intention to dedicate it.

COMMUNITY:

**We dedicate this labyrinth to spiritual awakening and reawakening.**

LEADER:

May springs of openness bubble forth here; may their energies kiss the feet of all who meander on the path.

COMMUNITY:

**We dedicate this labyrinth to spiritual awakening and reawakening.**

LEADER:

May those who come here perceive Your loveliness with all of who they are—their eyes, the soles of their feet, their ears, their breath, their heartbeats, their muscles, their minds, and their sense of balance.

COMMUNITY:

**We dedicate this labyrinth to spiritual awakening and reawakening.**

LEADER:

Thank You for welcoming the hopes that are brought here, as well as pains, questions, sighs, laughter, tears, and expressions of surprise.

COMMUNITY:

**We dedicate this labyrinth to spiritual awakening and reawakening.**

LEADER:

Thank You for gifting us with a sacred space where we can experience Your love as safety, rest, patience, kindness, goodness, hope, and healing.

COMMUNITY:

**We dedicate this labyrinth to spiritual awakening and reawakening.**

LEADER:

Out of our gratitude we each silently or verbally offer our own prayers of blessing and dedication for this labyrinth. (Long pause.)

COMMUNITY:

**We dedicate this labyrinth to spiritual awakening and reawakening.**

LEADER:

Amen!

## DEDICATION OF A CANVAS LABYRINTH IN A HOSPITAL SETTING

LEADER:

I am going to offer several prayers for this labyrinth. After each, I invite all of us to respond by repeating the following phrase, "We dedicate this labyrinth to the well-being of our community."

I invite you to cup your hands before you. Now imagine putting all your desires for this labyrinth in your hands until they are overflowing. As you now open your hands outward, send all the possibilities that you have imagined for this healing tool toward it.

If you would like, lift your hands toward the labyrinth as if you are sending blessings to it. Let us also offer our verbal blessing.

LEADER AND COMMUNITY:
**We dedicate this labyrinth to the well-being of our community.**

LEADER:
May this labyrinth be experienced as a pattern that nurtures health.

COMMUNITY:
**We dedicate this labyrinth to the well-being of our community.**

LEADER:
May those who arrive with hopelessness find the courage to step over the threshold into the possibilities of transformation.

COMMUNITY:
**We dedicate this labyrinth to the well-being of our community.**

LEADER:
May those who walk seeking wisdom, find it.

COMMUNITY:
**We dedicate this labyrinth to the well-being of our community.**

LEADER:
May those who travel the labyrinth's path carrying heavy burdens discover the ability to set those burdens down.

**COMMUNITY:**
**We dedicate this labyrinth to the well-being of our community.**

LEADER:
May the center be a place where those who are exhausted find rest, where those who are grieving receive comfort, and where those who are dejected encounter unexpected joy.

**COMMUNITY:**
**We dedicate this labyrinth to the well-being of our community.**

LEADER:
May those discovering new perspectives here, find the courage to act on them.

**COMMUNITY:**
**We dedicate this labyrinth to the well-being of our community.**

LEADER:
May all who experience the labyrinth discover Divine Love as their companion.

**COMMUNITY:**
**We dedicate this labyrinth to the well-being of our community.**

LEADER:
May it be so! Amen.

## MINNESOTA LABYRINTH NETWORK DEDICATION RITUALS

In Minnesota, a group of labyrinth enthusiasts meets three times a year to share information, encourage one another, and experience labyrinths together. It is not unusual for a member of the group to come with a newly constructed canvas labyrinth. When this happens, the group creates a spontaneous ritual to bless the labyrinth and its caretakers.

These dedications are very informal. They often involve the creator of the labyrinth walking to its center where she or he stands, sits, or kneels. Other group members circle the member in the center, sometimes laying hands on the person. Silent and spoken prayers for the ministry of the labyrinth are then offered by those who feel led to do so.

After the ritual, all are invited to walk the labyrinth and experience its unique gifts.

## PART EIGHT

# REFLECTING ON YOUR SACRED EXPLORATIONS

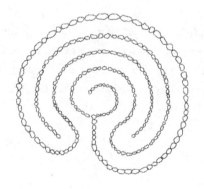

*These journal sheets are for your use each time you encounter the labyrinth. You may want to write in this book so you have a permanent record bound into this volume or you may want to photocopy the page that is speaking to you today so that you can use the sheets many times.*

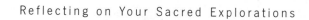 

## LABYRINTH JOURNAL

Date:

Location:

Relevant information:

Words and images that come in response to my labyrinth experience:

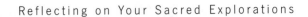 

**LABYRINTH JOURNAL**

Date:

Location:

Relevant information:

What I discovered as I prayed the labyrinth today:

## LABYRINTH JOURNAL

Date:

Location:

Relevant information:

What now?

## LABYRINTH JOURNAL

Date:

Location:

Relevant information:

What did I experience in the center?

What did I discover about moving on as I made my way out from the center?

## LABYRINTH JOURNAL

Date:

Location:

Relevant information:

What is my next step with the labyrinth?

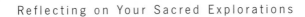 

**LABYRINTH JOURNAL**

Date:

Location:

Relevant information:

Use only images (no words) to continue to explore what began on the labyrinth:

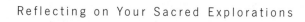 

## LABYRINTH JOURNAL

Date:

Location:

Relevant information:

The gifts of my labyrinth experience:

# PART NINE

## LEARNING MORE

## TRAINING PROGRAMS FOR LABYRINTH FACILITATORS

If you would like to receive training in labyrinth facilitation you may want to investigate these programs.

### Facilitator Training offered by the Rev. Dr. Lauren Artress

Veriditas. The Voice of the Labyrinth Movement.
www.veriditas.net; email: office@veriditas.net
Phone 415-561-2921, fax 415-561-2922

Taught by the Rev. Dr. Lauren Artress, this two-day intensive workshop will prepare you to introduce the labyrinth to others in a clear and effective way. The workshop is intended for those who have an ongoing relationship with the labyrinth, experience in leading small groups, and a vision of how they would like to use the labyrinth in their life's work.

### Intensive Labyrinth Training by Robert Ferré

Labyrinth Enterprises
www.labyrinth-enterprises.com
A training schedule is listed on the site.
Phone 800-873-9873

Robert describes this training as "an intensive, nonexperiential, stuff-them-full-of-information training for people already familiar with labyrinths who want to deepen their knowledge of history, sacred geometry, utilization, and construction of labyrinths."

### Sharing the Labyrinth: The Next Step

Wisdom Ways Center for Spirituality
www.wisdomwayscenter.org or wisdomways@csjstpaul.org
1890 Randolph Ave. St. Paul, MN 55105

Weekend workshop. Historical background, multiple patterns, labyrinth creation, movement and ritual, suggestions for use in diverse contexts, presentation options, and prayerful integration are included. Participants must have significant prior experience with labyrinths and have the intention of offering the labyrinth to the wider community.

## BIBLIOGRAPHY

Artress, Lauren. *Walking a Sacred Path: Rediscovering the Labyrinth as a Spiritual Tool.* New York: Riverhead Books, 1995.

Baker, Jonny, Steve Collins, et al. *The Prayer Path: A Christ-Centered Labyrinth Experience.* Loveland, CO, Group, 2001. (Booklet with paint can and compact disc).

Diehl, Huston. "Into the Maze of Self: The Protestant Transformation of the Image of the Labyrinth." *Journal of Medieval and Renaissance Studies* 16, no.2 (1986): 281–98.

Ellard, Peter. *The Theology of the School of Chartres and the Labyrinth of Chartres Cathedral.* Unpublished paper, American Academy of Religion, San Francisco, Calif., November, 1997.

Ferré, Robert. *Sacred Geometry: A lecture by Robert Ferré.* St. Louis: Labyrinth Enterprises, 2000.

Ferré, Robert. *Church Labyrinths: Questions and Answers Regarding the History, Relevance, and Use of Labyrinths in Churches.* St. Louis: Labyrinth Enterprises, 2001.

Ferré, Robert. *Constructing the Chartres Labyrinth: An Instruction Manual.* St. Louis: Labyrinth Enterprises, 2001.

Ferré, Robert. *Constructing the Classical Labyrinth: An Instruction Manual.* St. Louis: Labyrinth Enterprises, 2001.

Ferré, Robert. *Origin, Symbolism, and Design of the Chartres Labyrinth.* St. Louis: Labyrinth Enterprises, 2001.

Ferré, Robert. *Sacred Geometry, Chartres Cathedral, and the Labyrinth.* EpiCenter Tapes, The Labyrinth Society International Conference and Gathering, Atlanta, GA, November 2001.

Field, Robert. "Christian Pathways." *Mazes: Ancient and Modern.* Norfolk, England: Tarquin Publications, 1999, 32–41.

Geoffrion, Jill Kimberly Hartwell. *Praying the Labyrinth: A Journal for Spiritual Creativity.* Cleveland: Pilgrim Press, 1999.

Geoffrion, Jill Kimberly Hartwell. *Living the Labyrinth: 101 Paths to a Deeper Connection with the Sacred.* Cleveland: Pilgrim Press, 2000.

Geoffrion, Jill Kimberly Hartwell. *Labyrinth and Song of Songs.* Cleveland: Pilgrim Press, 2003.

Geoffrion, Jill Kimberly Hartwell. *Pondering the Labyrinth: Questions to Pray on the Path.* Cleveland: Pilgrim Press, 2003.

Geoffrion, Jill Kimberly Hartwell, and Elizabeth Catherine Nagel. *The Labyrinth and the Enneagram: Circling into Prayer.* Cleveland: Pilgrim Press, 2001.

Jones, Tony. "The Labyrinth." In *Soul Shaper.* El Cajon, Calif.: Youth Specialties, 2003. 143–51.

Kallstrom, Christine. *Children and the Labyrinth: Liturgical and Non-liturgical Uses.* Grand Prairie, Tex.: Alternative Learning Environments, 2001.

Kern, Hermann. *Through the Labyrinth: Designs and Meanings over 5,000 Years.* New York: Prestel, 2000.

Ketley-LaPorte, John and Odette. *Chartres: Le Labyrinthe Déchiffré*, France: Éditions Jean-Michel Garnier, 1997.

Saward, Jeff. *Ancient Labyrinths of the World*. Thundersley, England: Caerdroia, 1997.

Saward, Jeff. *Magical Paths: Labyrinths and Mazes in the 21st Century*. London: Mitchell Beazley, 2002.

Saward, Jeff. *Labyrinths and Mazes of the World*. New York: Lark Books, 2003.

Villette, Jean. *The Enigma of the Labyrinth*. St. Louis: One Way Press, 1995.

Westbrook, Walt. "The Labyrinth: A Pilgrimage Toward the Sacred." *Virginia Advocate* 169, no. 3 (Feb. 26, 2001): 3.

Wright, Craig. *The Maze and the Warrior: Symbols in Architecture, Theology, and Music*. Cambridge, Mass.: Harvard University Press, 2001.

## WEB RESOURCES

### Author's website

Deep Haven Labyrinths & Retreats
Jill Kimberly Hartwell Geoffrion
www.jillkhg.com

### Labyrinth Enterprises

Robert Ferré, Master Labyrinth Builder
Labyrinth construction and consultation; extensive internet links
128 Slocum St. Louis, MO 63119
800-873-9873, fax 888-873-9873
www.labyrinth-enterprises.com

### Veriditas, The Voice of the Labyrinth Movement

Lauren Artress, Founder
Labyrinth Events, Resources, and International Labyrinth Locator
The Presidio
1009 General Kennedy Ave., 1st floor
San Francisco, CA 94129
Phone 415-561-2921, fax 415-561-2922
www.veriditas.net

### World Wide Labyrinth Locator

A Joint Project of The Labyrinth Society and Veriditas
Can be accessed through wwll.veriditas.labyrinthsociety.org

*Other Titles by Jill Kimberly Hartwell Geoffrion from The Pilgrim Press*

## LABYRINTH AND THE SONG OF SONGS
A unique spiritual experience that cleverly intertwines traditional labyrinthine concepts and the entire Hebrew Scriptures love poem "Song of Songs." This is for the seasoned labyrinth aficionado who wants to take the next spiritual step. Features illustrations of the labyrinth of Chartres Cathedral and an original hymn.

0-8298-1539-2/112 pages/paper/$12.00

## PONDERING THE LABYRINTH
### Questions to Pray on the Path
This resource begins with answers to frequently asked questions about labyrinths and ending with questions to ponder for special reasons. Each chapter includes a reflection page with space to write your own questions.

0-8298-1575-9/112 pages/paper/$12.00

## PRAYING THE LABYRINTH
### A Journal for Spiritual Exploration
This book is a journal that leads readers into spiritual exercise of self-discovery through scripture selections, journaling questions, and poetry, with generous space for personal reflections.

0-8298-1343-8/128 pages/paper/$15.00

**To order these or any other books from The Pilgrim Press call or write to:**

The Pilgrim Press
700 Prospect Avenue East
Cleveland, Ohio 44115-1100

PHONE ORDERS: 800-537-3394 (M–F, 8:30 AM–4:30 PM ET)

FAX ORDERS: 216-736-2206

Please include shipping charges of $5.00 for the first book and $0.75 for each additional book.

Or order from our web site at www.thepilgrimpress.com.

*Prices subject to change without notice.*